Good for One
NIGHT OF

★ ★ ★ ★ ★ ★ ★ ★ ★ ★ ★ ★ ★ ★

EXPERT BABYSITTING

★ ★ ★ ★ ★ ★ ★ ★ ★ ★ ★ ★ ★ ★

Valid for one adorable child

Date: Call for appt.   **Time:** We'll work it out...
Hourly Rate:
Will accept hot chocolate, coffee, or hugs

Good for One
NIGHT OF

EXPERT BABYSITTING

Valid for one adorable child

Date: Call for appt.   **Time:** We'll work it out...
Hourly Rate:
Will accept hot chocolate, coffee, or hugs

Good for One
NIGHT OF

★★★★★★★★★★★★

EXPERT BABYSITTING

★★★★★★★★★★★★

Valid for one adorable child

Date: Call for appt. **Time:** We'll work it out...
Hourly Rate:
Will accept hot chocolate, coffee, or hugs

Good for One NIGHT OF

★ ★ ★ ★ ★ ★ ★ ★ ★ ★ ★ ★

EXPERT BABYSITTING

★ ★ ★ ★ ★ ★ ★ ★ ★ ★ ★ ★

Valid for one adorable child

Date: Call for appt. **Time:** We'll work it out...
Hourly Rate:
Will accept hot chocolate, coffee, or hugs

Good for One
NIGHT OF

EXPERT BABYSITTING

Valid for one adorable child

Date: Call for appt.   **Time:** We'll work it out...
Hourly Rate:
Will accept hot chocolate, coffee, or hugs

Good for One
NIGHT OF

★ ★ ★ ★ ★ ★ ★ ★ ★ ★ ★ ★ ★

EXPERT BABYSITTING

★ ★ ★ ★ ★ ★ ★ ★ ★ ★ ★ ★ ★

Valid for one adorable child

Date: Call for appt.   **Time:** We'll work it out...
Hourly Rate:
Will accept hot chocolate, coffee, or hugs

Good for One
NIGHT OF

★ ★ ★ ★ ★ ★ ★ ★ ★ ★ ★ ★

EXPERT BABYSITTING

★ ★ ★ ★ ★ ★ ★ ★ ★ ★ ★ ★

Valid for one adorable child

Date: Call for appt.   **Time:** We'll work it out...
Hourly Rate:
Will accept hot chocolate, coffee, or hugs

Good for One
NIGHT OF

EXPERT BABYSITTING

Valid for one adorable child

Date: Call for appt.   **Time:** We'll work it out...
Hourly Rate:
Will accept hot chocolate, coffee, or hugs

Good for One
NIGHT OF

★★★★★★★★★★★★★★★

EXPERT BABYSITTING

★★★★★★★★★★★★★★★

Valid for one adorable child

Date: Call for appt.   **Time:** We'll work it out...
Hourly Rate:
Will accept hot chocolate, coffee, or hugs

Good for One
NIGHT OF

★ ★ ★ ★ ★ ★ ★ ★ ★ ★ ★

EXPERT BABYSITTING

★ ★ ★ ★ ★ ★ ★ ★ ★ ★ ★

Valid for one adorable child

Date: Call for appt.   **Time:** We'll work it out...
Hourly Rate:
Will accept hot chocolate, coffee, or hugs

Good for One
NIGHT OF

★★★★★★★★★★★★★

EXPERT BABYSITTING

★★★★★★★★★★★★★

Valid for one adorable child

Date: Call for appt.　**Time:** We'll work it out...
Hourly Rate:
Will accept hot chocolate, coffee, or hugs

Good for One
NIGHT OF

EXPERT BABYSITTING

Valid for one adorable child

Date: Call for appt.   **Time:** We'll work it out...
Hourly Rate:
Will accept hot chocolate, coffee, or hugs

Good for One
NIGHT OF

EXPERT BABYSITTING

Valid for one adorable child

Date: Call for appt.   **Time:** We'll work it out...
Hourly Rate:
Will accept hot chocolate, coffee, or hugs

Good for One NIGHT OF

EXPERT BABYSITTING

Valid for one adorable child

Date: Call for appt.   **Time:** We'll work it out...
Hourly Rate:
Will accept hot chocolate, coffee, or hugs

Good for One
NIGHT OF

★ ★ ★ ★ ★ ★ ★ ★ ★ ★ ★ ★ ★ ★

EXPERT BABYSITTING

★ ★ ★ ★ ★ ★ ★ ★ ★ ★ ★ ★ ★ ★

Valid for one adorable child

Date: Call for appt.   **Time:** We'll work it out...
Hourly Rate:
Will accept hot chocolate, coffee, or hugs

Good for One
NIGHT OF

EXPERT BABYSITTING

Valid for one adorable child

Date: Call for appt.   **Time:** We'll work it out...
Hourly Rate:
Will accept hot chocolate, coffee, or hugs

Good for One
NIGHT OF

★ ★ ★ ★ ★ ★ ★ ★ ★ ★ ★ ★ ★ ★ ★

EXPERT BABYSITTING

★ ★ ★ ★ ★ ★ ★ ★ ★ ★ ★ ★ ★ ★ ★

Valid for one adorable child

Date: Call for appt.   **Time:** We'll work it out...
Hourly Rate:
Will accept hot chocolate, coffee, or hugs

Good for One
NIGHT OF

EXPERT BABYSITTING

Valid for one adorable child

Date: Call for appt. **Time:** We'll work it out...
Hourly Rate:
Will accept hot chocolate, coffee, or hugs

Good for One
NIGHT OF

EXPERT BABYSITTING

Valid for one adorable child

Date: Call for appt.   **Time:** We'll work it out...
Hourly Rate:
Will accept hot chocolate, coffee, or hugs

Good for One
NIGHT OF

EXPERT BABYSITTING

Valid for one adorable child

Date: Call for appt.   **Time:** We'll work it out...
Hourly Rate:
Will accept hot chocolate, coffee, or hugs

Good for One
NIGHT OF
EXPERT BABYSITTING
Valid for one adorable child

Date: Call for appt.   **Time:** We'll work it out...
Hourly Rate:
Will accept hot chocolate, coffee, or hugs

Good for One
NIGHT OF

★ ★ ★ ★ ★ ★ ★ ★ ★ ★ ★ ★ ★ ★

EXPERT BABYSITTING

★ ★ ★ ★ ★ ★ ★ ★ ★ ★ ★ ★ ★ ★

Valid for one adorable child

Date: Call for appt.　　**Time:** We'll work it out...
Hourly Rate:
Will accept hot chocolate, coffee, or hugs

Good for One
NIGHT OF

★ ★ ★ ★ ★ ★ ★ ★ ★ ★ ★ ★ ★

EXPERT BABYSITTING

★ ★ ★ ★ ★ ★ ★ ★ ★ ★ ★ ★ ★

Valid for one adorable child

Date: Call for appt.   **Time:** We'll work it out...
Hourly Rate:
Will accept hot chocolate, coffee, or hugs

Good for One
NIGHT OF

EXPERT BABYSITTING

Valid for one adorable child

Date: Call for appt.   **Time:** We'll work it out...
Hourly Rate:
Will accept hot chocolate, coffee, or hugs

Good for One
NIGHT OF

EXPERT BABYSITTING

Valid for one adorable child

Date: Call for appt.   **Time:** We'll work it out...
Hourly Rate:
Will accept hot chocolate, coffee, or hugs

Good for One
NIGHT OF

★★★★★★★★★★★★★★★★

EXPERT BABYSITTING

★★★★★★★★★★★★★★★★

Valid for one adorable child

Date: Call for appt. **Time:** We'll work it out...
Hourly Rate:
Will accept hot chocolate, coffee, or hugs

Good for One
NIGHT OF

★ ★ ★ ★ ★ ★ ★ ★ ★ ★ ★

EXPERT BABYSITTING

★ ★ ★ ★ ★ ★ ★ ★ ★ ★ ★

Valid for one adorable child

Date: Call for appt. **Time:** We'll work it out...
Hourly Rate:
Will accept hot chocolate, coffee, or hugs

Good for One
NIGHT OF

⭐⭐⭐⭐⭐⭐⭐⭐⭐⭐⭐⭐

EXPERT BABYSITTING

⭐⭐⭐⭐⭐⭐⭐⭐⭐⭐⭐⭐

Valid for one adorable child

Date: Call for appt.   **Time:** We'll work it out...
Hourly Rate:
Will accept hot chocolate, coffee, or hugs

Good for One
NIGHT OF

⭐⭐⭐⭐⭐⭐⭐⭐⭐⭐⭐⭐

EXPERT BABYSITTING

⭐⭐⭐⭐⭐⭐⭐⭐⭐⭐⭐⭐

Valid for one adorable child

Date: Call for appt.   **Time:** We'll work it out...
Hourly Rate:
Will accept hot chocolate, coffee, or hugs

Good for One
NIGHT OF

EXPERT BABYSITTING

Valid for one adorable child

Date: Call for appt.   **Time:** We'll work it out...
Hourly Rate:
Will accept hot chocolate, coffee, or hugs

Good for One
NIGHT OF

★ ★ ★ ★ ★ ★ ★ ★ ★ ★ ★ ★

EXPERT BABYSITTING

★ ★ ★ ★ ★ ★ ★ ★ ★ ★ ★ ★

Valid for one adorable child

Date: Call for appt.   **Time:** We'll work it out...
Hourly Rate:
Will accept hot chocolate, coffee, or hugs

Good for One NIGHT OF

★★★★★★★★★★★★★★★★★★

EXPERT BABYSITTING

★★★★★★★★★★★★★★★★★★

Valid for one adorable child

Date: Call for appt.   **Time:** We'll work it out...
Hourly Rate:
Will accept hot chocolate, coffee, or hugs

Good for One
NIGHT OF

★ ★ ★ ★ ★ ★ ★ ★ ★ ★ ★ ★

EXPERT BABYSITTING

★ ★ ★ ★ ★ ★ ★ ★ ★ ★ ★ ★

Valid for one adorable child

Date: Call for appt.   **Time:** We'll work it out...
Hourly Rate:
Will accept hot chocolate, coffee, or hugs

Good for One
NIGHT OF

★ ★ ★ ★ ★ ★ ★ ★ ★ ★ ★ ★ ★ ★

EXPERT BABYSITTING

★ ★ ★ ★ ★ ★ ★ ★ ★ ★ ★ ★ ★ ★

Valid for one adorable child

Date: Call for appt.   **Time:** We'll work it out...
Hourly Rate:
Will accept hot chocolate, coffee, or hugs

Good for One
NIGHT OF

EXPERT BABYSITTING

Valid for one adorable child

Date: Call for appt.   **Time:** We'll work it out...
Hourly Rate:
Will accept hot chocolate, coffee, or hugs

Good for One **NIGHT OF**

EXPERT BABYSITTING

Valid for one adorable child

Date: Call for appt.   **Time:** We'll work it out...
Hourly Rate:
Will accept hot chocolate, coffee, or hugs

Good for One
NIGHT OF

EXPERT BABYSITTING

Valid for one adorable child

Date: Call for appt.   **Time:** We'll work it out...
Hourly Rate:
Will accept hot chocolate, coffee, or hugs

Good for One
NIGHT OF
EXPERT BABYSITTING
Valid for one adorable child

Date: Call for appt.   **Time:** We'll work it out...
Hourly Rate:
Will accept hot chocolate, coffee, or hugs

Good for One
NIGHT OF

EXPERT BABYSITTING

Valid for one adorable child

Date: Call for appt.   **Time:** We'll work it out...
Hourly Rate:
Will accept hot chocolate, coffee, or hugs

Good for One
NIGHT OF

EXPERT BABYSITTING

Valid for one adorable child

Date: Call for appt.   **Time:** We'll work it out...
Hourly Rate:
Will accept hot chocolate, coffee, or hugs

Good for One **NIGHT OF**

★★★★★★★★★★★★★

EXPERT BABYSITTING

★★★★★★★★★★★★★

Valid for one adorable child

Date: Call for appt.   **Time:** We'll work it out...
Hourly Rate:
Will accept hot chocolate, coffee, or hugs

Good for One
NIGHT OF

★ ★ ★ ★ ★ ★ ★ ★ ★ ★ ★ ★ ★

EXPERT BABYSITTING

★ ★ ★ ★ ★ ★ ★ ★ ★ ★ ★ ★

Valid for one adorable child

Date: Call for appt.   **Time:** We'll work it out...
Hourly Rate:
Will accept hot chocolate, coffee, or hugs

Good for One
NIGHT OF

EXPERT BABYSITTING

Valid for one adorable child

Date: Call for appt.   **Time:** We'll work it out...
Hourly Rate:
Will accept hot chocolate, coffee, or hugs

Good for One
NIGHT OF

★★★★★★★★★★★★★

EXPERT BABYSITTING

★★★★★★★★★★★★★

Valid for one adorable child

Date: Call for appt.　**Time:** We'll work it out...
Hourly Rate:
Will accept hot chocolate, coffee, or hugs

Good for One
NIGHT OF

★★★★★★★★★★★★★★★★

EXPERT BABYSITTING

★★★★★★★★★★★★★★★★

Valid for one adorable child

Date: Call for appt.　**Time:** We'll work it out...
Hourly Rate:
Will accept hot chocolate, coffee, or hugs

Good for One
NIGHT OF

EXPERT BABYSITTING

Valid for one adorable child

Date: Call for appt.   **Time:** We'll work it out...
Hourly Rate:
Will accept hot chocolate, coffee, or hugs

Good for One
NIGHT OF

★ ★ ★ ★ ★ ★ ★ ★ ★ ★ ★ ★ ★

EXPERT BABYSITTING

★ ★ ★ ★ ★ ★ ★ ★ ★ ★ ★ ★ ★

Valid for one adorable child

Date: Call for appt.   **Time:** We'll work it out...
Hourly Rate:
Will accept hot chocolate, coffee, or hugs

Good for One
NIGHT OF

EXPERT BABYSITTING

Valid for one adorable child

Date: Call for appt.   **Time:** We'll work it out...
Hourly Rate:
Will accept hot chocolate, coffee, or hugs

Good for One
NIGHT OF

★ ★ ★ ★ ★ ★ ★ ★ ★ ★ ★

EXPERT BABYSITTING

★ ★ ★ ★ ★ ★ ★ ★ ★ ★ ★

Valid for one adorable child

Date: Call for appt.　　**Time:** We'll work it out...
Hourly Rate:
Will accept hot chocolate, coffee, or hugs

Made in the USA
Columbia, SC
27 July 2021